IMPOSSIBLE BELONGING

IMPOSSIBLE BELONGING

MAYA PINDYCK

2021 PHILIP LEVINE PRIZE FOR POETRY

Selected by
Carmen Giménez Smith

ANHINGA PRESS
TALLAHASSEE, FLORIDA 2023

Cover art: Tamar Ettun, "The Yellow Who Wants," Installation view
        at Uppsala konstmuseum, 2016 (https://tamaettun.com).
        Photograph by Q Image.
Cover design: Carol Lynne Knight
Author photo: Beowulf Sheehan
Text design and production: Carol Lynne Knight
Type Styles: Titles are set in Neue Kabel; text is set in Minion Pro

Library of Congress Cataloging-in-Publication Data
"Impossible Belonging" by Maya Pindyck, First Edition
ISBN – 978-1-934695-76-0
Library of Congress Cataloging Card Number – 2022937450

Anhinga Press Inc. is dedicated wholly to the
publication and appreciation of fine poetry and other literary genres.

For personal orders, catalogs and information write to:
Anhinga Press
P.O. Box 3665
Tallahassee, Florida 32315
Website: www.anhingapress.org
Email: info@anhinga.org

Published in the United States
by Anhinga Press
Tallahassee, Florida
First Edition, 2023

for my mother & her mother—

&

for Noa & Alma

THE PHILIP LEVINE PRIZE FOR POETRY

The annual competition for the Philip Levine Prize for Poetry is sponsored and administered by the M.F.A. Program in Creative Writing at California State University, Fresno.

2021
Maya Pindyck
Impossible Belonging
Selected by Carmen Giménez Smith

2020
E.C. Belli
A Sleep That Is Not Our Sleep
Selected by Cathy Park Hong

2019
Steven Kleinman
Life Cycle of a Bear
Selected by C. G. Hanzlicek

2018
Mark Irwin
Shimmer
Selected by C. G. Hanzlicek

2017
Tina Mozelle Braziel
Known by Salt
Selected by C. G. Hanzlicek

2016
Rachel Rinehart
The Church in the Plains
Selected by Peter Everwine

2015
Andrea Jurjević
Small Crimes
Selected by C. G. Hanzlicek

2014
Christine Poreba
Rough Knowledge
Selected by Peter Everwine

2013
Chelsea Wagenaar
Mercy Spurs the Bone
Selected by Philip Levine

2012
Barbara Brinson Curiel
Mexican Jenny and Other Poems
Selected by Cornelius Eady

2011
Ariana Nadia Nash
Instructions for Preparing Your Skin
Selected by Denise Duhamel

2010
Lory Bedikian
The Book of Lamenting
Selected by Brian Turner

2009
Sarah Wetzel
Bathsheba Transatlantic
Selected by Garrett Hongo

2008
Shane Seely
The Snowbound House
Selected by Dorianne Laux

2007
Neil Aitken
The Lost Country of Sight
Selected by C. G. Hanzlicek

2006
Lynn Aarti Chandhok
The View from Zero Bridge
Selected by Corrinne Clegg Hales

2005
Roxane Beth Johnson
Jubilee
Selected by Philip Levine

2002
Steven Gehrke
The Pyramids of Malpighi
Selected by Philip Levine

2001
Fleda Brown
Breathing In, Breathing Out
Selected by Philip Levine

CONTENTS

ACKNOWLEDGMENTS

I am grateful to the editors of the publications in which these poems first appeared, sometimes in different forms:

Barrow Street: "The Body After, the Body Before"

Bennington Review: "Notes on Pears"

Granta (Hebrew edition): Translations to Hebrew of "Boy," "To the Israeli Woman Who Worried Her Daughter's Doll Spoke Arabic," "Transparent," "The Israeli Schoolgirl Forgets"

Los Angeles Review: "Boy"

Massachusetts Review: "The United States: An Introduction"

MAYDAY Magazine: "What We Want"

Ovenbird Poetry: "To the Pigeon Caught Inside Union Station"

Pleiades: "It Was the Year of the Dog"

Quarterly West: "Half Poem"

Seneca Review: "Violet Blossoms with Guidelines," "Alma, in the morning," "Parental Error in the Anthropocene," "Ode to the Subway Door Scratches," "regrets, upon hearing of her death"

SWWIM Every Day: "Present Tense" (featured on The Slowdown podcast)

Tablet: "The Photograph," "Reading the Crease"

Tether: "The Israeli Schoolgirl Forgets"

Thank you to the National Endowment for the Arts for the gift of resources and support. And to Moore College of Art & Design for the professional support to carry out this work.

Deep gratitude to Mai Der Vang and Jefferson Beavers at California State University, Fresno, for helping to move this book into the world, and to the readers of the Philip Levine Prize. Carmen Giménez, to be chosen by you is a huge honor. Thank you. To the wonderful folks at Anhinga: Lynne Knight, Kristine Snodgrass & Amber Lunderman, many thanks for your editorial vision and all your work on this book.

Friends, family, students, teachers: Thank you, each, for your love and support. You nourish and open my life. This collection owes specific gratitude to Kaveh Bassiri and Jennie Panchy for generous reads of earlier drafts. Rachel Eliza Griffiths, for your words and friendship and spirit. And to my writing/art communities intersecting with the making of this book: J. Mae Barizo, Francisco Eraso, Tamar Ettun, Leora Fridman, Eshé All Day Hues, Ellie Lobovitz, Maxwell Neely-Cohen, and Sarah Riggs, for your caring responses to poems in this book. Taije Silverman and Robert Whitehead for evenings writing together. To rosenclaire & the workshoppers for continued study, particularly Carla Repice, Dorota Mytych, Reem Rahim, Jessica Houston, and Angela Ellsworth for collaborations that seeded thoughts from which many of these poems grew. Claudine Thomas, Daniel Tucker, Leigh Gallagher, and Mariam Williams, for your keen eyes on my writing. And Victoria Restler, Jessica Hamlin, and Asilia Franklin-Phipps: these pages thrive alongside our collective work & conversations.

Suzanne Gardinier, Charles O. Hartman, Marie Howe, Kate Knapp Johnson, D. Nurkse, Vijay Seshadri, the late Tom Lux, and Ruth Vinz, my poetry teachers: continued gratitude.

Nurit, Bob, Talia & Shira, family of wildflowers & hyenas, I am the luckiest.

Tyler, thank you for this life together, inch by inch, row by row.

Noa and Alma, my hearts. Thank you for you.

With whose blood were my eyes crafted?
— Donna Haraway

*

Ruins are relics.
The lineage being of little importance, we're related to them.
— Etel Adnan

IMPOSSIBLE BELONGING

*

WINTER DAY TRANSCRIPTION

Once there was a forest
and the forest had a wolf
who waited for girls to pass by —

One girl came
and the wolf ate her

and she saw his lungs
and no bones

but then she climbed the bones
and the bones
appeared.

She died in the wolf's body.

She got out before she died.

When she got back in —
                         well, she didn't go *back* in —

She died at the entrance.

BOY

Someone made the school a plaque
of names. I find the one I wanted

for my never-son: bronze prince
stirring a pond with all his brothers.

My family came here from a country
I am not allowed to visit

even though its spices fill my cabinet.
My other family never made it.

I once walked a field
covering their bodies. Wildflowers

& grasses. Here, the story of a line
of children shot in the schoolyard.

Here, Manek's hairbrush shop.
What I can't wrap my head around

is the story of the boy playing ball
by the hole where they hid —

how he ratted them out to a soldier.
I try to imagine how that boy

grew. To love his own
boys, only, playing hide & seek

in the sun? And is that boy's boy
a boy who now trains to turn

a life lethal, to pull a trigger
out of fear, or rage, or duty?

I don't know, but I think it's the same boy
stammering history & now & here — boy

who waves in the night to be seen.

IT WAS THE YEAR OF THE DOG

so I removed the unthawed
placenta from my freezer
two years too late
and instead of burying it
with my moon blood beneath the dogwood
as the four white women advised
I flung it far into the mouth
of a rabid hound
searching for scraps of bone,
anything — my body. *Violent*
said the women from their hedges.
Soil is a more spiritual choice. Shit
crusting my daughter's flesh, and the howling
upturning everything we've buried — the dead
stars alight with watching: you are
my only one

TO THE ISRAELI WOMAN WHO WORRIED HER DAUGHTER'S DOLL SPOKE ARABIC

But it was not necessarily Arabic —

more like a chortle of vowels begging for companionship,
or maybe to be left alone.

But she loves her doll and the button on his chest.

But it was your twin flowing out his mouth
into the valley & the sea
that laps your spongy tongue.

But it was necessarily Arabic.

And though my grandfather arrived
to Palestine from Aleppo, you said he would cry
if I ever married an Arab.

But isn't language how we come to love a home
that baffles the scaffolds making us

we? But your children — look at them —
build a fort and inside it share an omelet.

But you named them Light and Variation on Light.

But this room already forgot
whose idea, whose hands, whose

before. But the orange tree.

But the string of sounds beads a rosary,
pulling spheres across your skin.

But our blood, inside its tribe, stains
this place we petrify.

PARENTAL ERROR IN THE ANTHROPOCENE

My daughter wants to touch a real-life flower.

The kind where purple smells of summer's chest
heaving dewy breath. Obsessed

with accidental death, I grab her grasping hand —
Don't pull! — to teach her something about power.

The flower seems unbothered
but I cling to my good lesson:

One stalk yanked, a world gone.

Yawn.

I can already feel my words
turning against us — her hand suddenly

unsure how to touch.

VIOLET BLOSSOMS WITH GUIDELINES

After Hilma af Klint

Do not hurt another, the field
empty of flowers says
beneath which my family's bones soften
though never to the likes of their surrounding
worms. Curious how memory turns
to march in squares, atoms away
from today: unnamed by the news, a girl
violet with loss — her only sister
rubble-deep — drones on.

THE PHOTOGRAPH

For years I wished to be my mother in the photograph:

short-haired soldier dressed in khaki,
aiming her rifle at some imaginary
terrorist, sepia-toned
like the photograph itself.

The photograph's ability to summon
a threat became my definition of *feminist:*
a woman enacting a man's violence
with better precision than he can envision.

Our friend from the kibbutz grew to be
the first woman to fly a fighter plane for the army.

We swelled with pride hearing stories of her
fogging commanders with engine smoke.

Girl power meant flexing the nation's bicep
to prove its dream of equality.
I can do anything.
Kill anyone.

In the photograph, my mother's eye

meets the rifle's scope. Her daughters,
though we will not serve,
harden from her hope.

Now, a woman, I have chosen
the warrior's path: black walnut tree
releasing toxicity with tools belonging

to my own body, greening
& invisible to any
I.

HALF POEM

After the war all that remains
reads as half scribbles of the half dead

language. I stop to eat an empanada,
half butterfly, by the lapping waves

and salivating dogs. Let the poem be the place
we touch our other halves, somewhere

between the parcels carried,
her cotton bag & face — *Who is it you*

remember? On 9th Street half a sandwich
bares its chest to the public.

No sparrow. No hungry child. Only
half a gesture to feed the people

this country's long forgotten.
Half a history spreads over

our dining table in waxy scratches,
its grooves undoing the swinging

door. Like you've lived here before.
Let the poem be the place

the ghost half rages at how
we've made of the tree —

rain, soil, light — a weapon
with which to close upon

the quiet, half-lit slivers
longing for nothing.

YOU ARE A WITNESS TO WHAT YOU DON'T SEE

The heart: old tugboat,
its motor sore & somewhere

a sail
pulling me back to where

we wailed:
Egypt, Syria,

no man's land
peopled & loved.

Remember our country
banning the book noting

our refusal to see.
Remember this compass

mapping our last past.

THE SUITCASE

The woman named my mother wheels
her dead mother's suitcase
up & down the streets of Boston's Copley Square,
catching strangers' eyes —
Would you like to meet my mother?
Oblivious to, or maybe relishing, the dissonance
between a smartly dressed white woman
wafting Shalimar perfume & this
startling question, she asks, dying
for connection. Each person
pretends not to hear, but anyway, my mother lays
the suitcase flat to pavement,
unclicks its buckle, zips it open. Pulls out
one petite wool sweater after another,
a glass giraffe unnested from its shelf in Maoz-Aviv,
a pair of socks freshly ironed, empty
tubes of Clinique face cream,
a pink hair curler.
She splays each artifact,
as if preserved in invisible amber,
on the sidewalk, before returning
everything to its case.
My mother begins again,
stopping passersby to notice
these fundamental elements.
By coincidence, my mother bumps into
her optometrist, who greets her
with a smile & extended hand,
certain she is the woman he knows.
When she asks the question again,
without a flicker of recognition,
he moves on. My mother watches him
with eyes that were not there
to see her own mother die in her homeland
without her. My mother carries her

mother's dead in the suitcase,
all of them,
hiding in forests or in sacks of potatoes,
the ones found by the young
boy who, a good boy, told a soldier
who, a good soldier, shot them on the spot.
My mother carries with her mother
the entire town of Boyberik,
the smidge of Yiddish left over,
the piles of sisters dragged from gas chambers
for burning. No wonder my mother
finally finds herself among today's wretched
warming their hands by a puff of steam
circling the sewer's grate,
seeing her for all that she has lost.
Yes, they reply, *we would like to meet your mother.*
No wonder she slams shut the suitcase,
seeing for once where she is & who
she could become, deciding at that moment
to name the wheeling of the suitcase *Art*
& to return to the living
who, each day, together,
practice forgetting.

EARLY LIGHT

I raised the wrong hand
to my heart before the flag
in Ms. Kagan's Kindergarten class,
prompting her to stick a Band-Aid
on my right pointer finger
to help me remember —
that is how this country got built
inside me — my lefty tendencies
strong since I could first fling
a plastic block's cocky solidity
across the alphabet carpet —
and how I learned to stand
in obedience, pledging allegiance
to the high fabric
secure upon its pole:
innocuous prop revealing
nothing of the hands
that dreamed it
up

THE THIRD YEAR

You have to touch the fire of letters.

If it burns? If I stay
broken on the alphabet?

Tomorrow the pages will be packed.

But I am the wind, & you
the faces of the moon.

In the living bedroom, I am everything.

Love honks its song:
Marcell, Marcell, Marcell, Marcell —

In nightfall I saw the sun fall
blue & pink — no letters.

THE UNITED STATES: AN INTRODUCTION

While we compare sex stories,
flaunt lines crossed —

a married man — a loading dock —
a stripper in the state that pays its strippers best —

the fireflies do their thing,
blinking neon hearts,

and peaches and chard
heat up on the grill

soon to bear the rack's lines
across their bodies.

(Burned histories
served on white plates.)

— One last story
wobbles into the garden

to name a day kindness failed:
A simple *yes*

to a cruel word said about a girl
whose ear pressed the door.

This our storyteller cannot forget
This

her shoulders hold like statues
of men on horses raising the day

someone died to put them there,
aloft and galloping over

those accumulated pains
hidden in the hoof's soft stain.

WHAT WE WANT

Peaches overflow the given
bowl: a gift from two lovers

no longer in love. One
remarried a restaurant hostess.
The other found new life in Connecticut.

It's cold for the first time this October.

My coat fails my neck —
I clutch its collar close and slip
my fingers through the knit, wanting

what wool wants: some famished moth
to prove its worth and eat and birth.

A THEORY OF ART

When I was eighteen, my favorite teacher said I reminded him
of his favorite teacher, Jane — Jewish, pale & skinny, like me,
& how he still carried with him that crush. Would I like
to write him sticky letters with terrible secrets?
Up to me, really. At that age, I believed
I was special & had a soul men wanted
to hold. If I didn't let them, would I
disappear? I drew out the fishing line,
fashioned myself Mermaid Fatale.
For years, he came in my dreams
& I imagined his apartment
a clean white cube
built for hanging
one perfect
painting.

CONSTRUCTIONS OF GREEN

lime souring the mango boat

army fatigue
energized by its false claim to nature

a boy's color I'm told

goblin skin

the garden's oversized cucumber
yanked by old hands

half of Christmas

one fourth of the Palestinian flag

somewhere between truth & proof
of life

deep-pine apron

In the video I appear to have a blinking problem

emerald

"green with envy"

a white woman paling & close
to hurling

she forgot to water the plants

REFRAIN

Our neighbors throw their mattress to the street.

Spring clings to its surface — buds, wisps,
a lone twig. The next day

someone's splayed purse has joined the party.
A dog's leather mouth.

And the next day —

Who believes in the pattering of patterns
taut with wires? Who among us wears this skin
best?

At night we sleep with one pillow between us,
and our dreams, they say, also pass between us,

arduous particles dragging depressions
from one body to the next — (I should have been
more careful) — changing chemistries

as a horse drug can change a sex
from womanly wood to manly water, and I want
an air mattress

to throw down myself
over this swollen city, beneath the empty
tree, barely dressed in trash, sprouting

plastic gasps — where we
sleep in public agony.

NOTES ON PEARS

Pears belong to no one.

Not the man who owns this home
nor his biting child.

Rusting skins brim
sweet verses.

Pears fill our mouths.

Surrounding pears: a wooden table,
stone plate, ceramic eye — remember

someone made of you
vibration.

One pear balances her crescent booty
on other pears.

Pears huddle in secret.

Sleepless, pears
know something of war.

Pears can rest anywhere.

Our ears hear pears
falling, chewed, or sliced.

Six pears soften in the night.

AGE

You know that blanket that is the ocean?

The one where you can only see
legs sticking out and feet
and shoes that look like sandals?

That's where I was when the monster came.

He swooped into my room with his name:
Age — pronounced *Aji* — meaning *wind* —
and threatened to take me from myself.

He became both closet and hanger,
flapping my quietest dress
in uncompromising positions.

Only when I lifted my bodies to the monster,
when I bent my knees and my legs and the blanket rose,
only then did he walk away.

Human again
and closing the door behind him.

LETTER TO A LINOLEUM TILE

O Bearer of the Unmistakable
Poor Man's Marble:

I see you everywhere, forever
 — motels, schools, banks, offices —
burying your face in our feet.

At the risk of rudeness, I am writing to ask
how often you get laid
to grout & who makes you
believe an antidote to life exists?

Institutional you, you
work hard but cannot freeze
my last animal memory.

MY GRANDMOTHER RETURNS AS A DEER

Close to home, she nuzzles
my footie pajamas. *Kind deer! Your frosty spots
pearl my eyes.* Honeyed tea

steams our mugs, nestled around
the usual platter of salty olives, sugared almonds,
velvety dates, among which we sit,

thunderous, under a quiet lake. Spied on
by the deer's queer gaze.

THE BURDEN

When remembering came too hard
for the man who sunk deep in the down
comforter of erasure — *What plan? What day?*
When the time, that for forty years nodded
him asleep & let him rise without seeing
the hands slice the bread & fold the girl's leggings
stopped — when the woman was gone
& the laughter followed: *Mr. Mom* —
It was too much & the flowers
came in not-enough droves
& the sympathy cards failed to convey
the burden of waking in a country
built to make you forget
the dignity of running warm water
over the plate's back, the slow draw
of a sponge disappearing the hummus smear
for a future hunger.

THE AMERICAN DREAM

of wheat light streaked
by clouds, lavender, turning old
industry alert with promise, and projects
housing the (unseen) mother's waking
flood with morning hue the hour
before work begins — the punching
of punch cards, in and out.

TO THE PIGEON CAUGHT INSIDE UNION STATION

You've reclaimed a gods-eye view
from the beam that splits this station's sky
in two — & as soon as we spot you,
you take off, swoop left, over Gate I,
past the blue banner that points with white arrows
to where a person can find a garage, or a bus,
& I want to touch the place your feet just touched—
there, on the water-streaked surface impossible
to reach, near your seared shadow — oh!
dark flutter, side right, stutters my heart
as you stroll across the floor in those old
pink socks, wings tucked in their usual part,
like you've lived here forever. To find
a way out is another bird's endeavor.

WITH MY LITTLE EYE I SPY

Noa packing the pages with pictures

Mango pocking her pearly chin

Exposed scaffolds passing as kings

A moth, frantic to find a patch of wall

Free of death's residue

The lake we'll never touch

Your hand, bigger than I remember

Your tongue snaking back

National magazines fanning the table

Expanse of land blurring by

Invisible commuters cracking

Hard candies shattering

Mouths violet

POEM FOR WHITE PEOPLE

> And what does the we-bird see with
> who has lost its I's?   — Audre Lorde

When my friend didn't acknowledge me
in her new book of poetry, I cried for two days straight,
sobbing in the shower, weeping in my bed,
eyes puffed between pillows.
I drafted her a letter about how hurt I felt
not to be named among her sea of beloveds
& speculated it was because I failed to show up
when she needed friends most & how sorry I was about that,
or maybe I was deluded about our closeness,
or maybe, I bit with desperate teeth, just maybe
there's a rift between who she calls kin in private
& who she publicly embraces — *a fucking performance!* —
my ego raged. Still, I insisted, I was proud to know her
& proud to celebrate her new book. Bravo.
This was after Amy Cooper performed the white damsel
threatened by the black birdwatcher, after a police officer
kneeled on George Floyd's neck past his last breath,
after cops shot Breonna Taylor in her bedroom,
after the murders of countless unnamed
because we don't have the footage to feel it.
My white misery choked me back to the dead,
lonely bone I was, dead & needing death to prove my worth.
So, this is how it works, I thought. If I stay this white,
I'll always be a General urging my bodies into monument,
bronzing time to freeze my pose. All for my name
etched beneath the horse's feet, commanding a reader.
Later that week I protested in the streets
with all the people who are everyone's people —
crowd of cardboard & smoke rising — & I
could feel what I could become: organ
no longer my own, alive in swell & shatter, rolling
to flames — our names & the horses we are

loosened from our saddles. Imagine our hands
making without us, what we might be
flowering with the fires we feel
when not so damn white. Each night
the moon cackles, meshuggeneh hyena,
doing its own thing, making its own light.

KARINA'S VIRUS

Wrong was everything.
Beds were outside.
Cars self-drove their bodies
backwards. The backyard
broke its starlings.
This morning the mayor
announced the virus can jump
higher than six feet
and we should all stock up
on meat. A girl
this morning made a book
about the courage it takes
not to anger a bee.
It ended with her decision
to never take down a tree.
It ended with her marrying
the dead leaves nuzzling
the living. *Thank you for staying
still.* This morning what
belies human surprise
thrives.

BIRTHDAY

On the hottest day of summer, my mother & father
chase each other with meringue pies on paper plates.
I remember the smack of cream on my face
& crying because I never saw them so dangerous,
so inside their bodies like that: my mother
howling up the driveway as my father's pie hits
the threadbare blue of her back. I try to hide
between two bikes in the garage, but their laughter
fills the sky & the air — & I am spared nowhere.

THE BODY AFTER, THE BODY BEFORE

Doubled over, doubled
back, squat ghost, you appear

twice in each of the landlord's two
visions — first in the hallway,

then in the living room, by the orange
bookshelf tight with spines.

I sleep better knowing
you could be the afternoon light cracking up

the window where my daughter laughs
and points at the portrait of you

at forty (though I wish this picture
didn't remind me so much of a president,

or a king), and I wonder now why
your body in its last months, weeks, grasses

rained with Arabic song after song after
song — *What once was was and is*

no longer — shimmering in seas
as you sat in your black leather armchair

facing the TV's floating soap
operas and sitcoms, why those words

came over you in that language
and not the others: Hebrew, Spanish, Russian,

or the small swath of English you pocketed,
why your hands shook with such joy

at your own singing of those songs,
the only songs now that mattered

after you built your life
sharpening this country's teeth.

THE MANNEQUIN

On Christmas Eve we took a cab to Jaffa Port
for a tour of the city's oldest churches
and rolled by the lit inside of a clothing store
where a mannequin perched: white, headless
woman in a pine-needle robe scarred with holly.
Ornaments sparkling red dizzied her chest.
This, on the thin road snaking by Abouelafia
and its smell of sesame breads. Our driver
gestured at the mannequin, grinning,
as if to affirm some blood, some clay,
that makes us cousins: *That's the nicest thing*
the Arabs have ever done. I said
nothing, and I am still ashamed of how
I shut his back door with my usual force.

THE ISRAELI SCHOOLGIRL FORGETS

her tribe for one
second before
the flag

unshadows
the names
of soldiers

carving
the door.
Those killed

have a killer
to blame.
When her eyes

meet the boy's
the names
disappear.

Or return.
Her head turns
to the watching

boy, his hands
at his sides.
The only hands

he has.
The only
hands he has.

A new way
to bind bodies
begs making

— blue
of the torn
button-down,

wrong blue,
the flag's stitches
falling —

TRANSPARENT

My mother thinks she's losing me
as I become more transparent —

Promise me you won't write another poem
bashing my home.

Eyes closed
the woman on the Q train
rests alert hands on her purse.

She reminds me of my mother's mother
offering us sisters in a browning glass
mint leaves boiling into tea.

A plate of dates from the newest country's oldest city.

The poet said that to lose one's identity is to become
more transparent. I think she means that to lose
one's mother is an imaginable thing.

I don't identify as white, said the white woman at the conference.

White is not a color, said my daughter.

I return but do not know from where to return.

The waters inside me keep running, calling me to a borderless state.

My mother thinks she's losing me — our country
beckons. Each time, I find myself
quelling its ghosts: the rabbi
who told the people in our village not to leave their homes.

We listened & died while he left just in time.

The power he yields greases my hair. Beware.

SOUTH STREET

If children with homes can turn homeless
like the woman outside Whole Foods with open palms
asking for mother — for money — the woman
we give $10 to & who replies   I love you —
does that mean, my daughter worries, she too
will one day live in the wide & jawless streets?
I offer no certainty & say to her — the woman —
I love you — she asks how it would feel to tell her
she is beautiful — how would she feel,
the woman, my daughter, hearing that?
She is a girl who could become a version
of herself fifty years ago or fifty years from now
drawing one line from one mouth to yours.

CALL & RESPONSE

Between the living
& the dining rooms
the woman screams

& the girl who hears asks me
to ask the woman to please stop screaming
to please stop begging for her mother's water
a sip of her mother —

I am thirsty, she tells the girl
but what can we do? Trace her back
to the Jew dressed in gingham
who killed herself in our kitchen
after the war? I cannot hear her

as my breasts fill & let down a river made
for another mouth.

ALMA, IN THE MORNING

and afternoon — even evening — erases
the word before we write it

leaves in its space
the half-whine of trying
to roll to one side
just to touch
the knitted octopus's open iris

all the time, Alma
revives saba's seawater eyes
twinkling before his final move:
slide queen to eat

pawn. Alma, always
cries for want of milk
and smells of wheat and sheep
grazing in damp fields where Alma sighs

sweet sleep, her working mouth
the motor that makes the river

each hour we burrow deep
the lint lined chin
to undo the burn

— *return*

"AIR HOLDS EVERYONE VISIBLE OR NOT"

Where do you find them?

A child's dress peeking out
Afghan rubble, a woman's arm
between a bulldozer's spokes,
the beggar wobbling on a stair
in the town square. I've lost everything

I could see. Everyone,
wildflowers, leaning their brown faces
over the border's edge.

Amir, I wanted to name you,
but you slipped into the folds
of your mother's skirt
& disappeared — a hand's imprint

made of the stillness
of stars.

AN OLD TESTAMENT

the jews put god in jail
for being in the night
without them

& for believing
the oil burned for ten nights, not eight

& even though one jew was mean
& another jew was mean
& another

they helped god stand up in the dirt

so that god could become 100 years old
then infinity years old
then back to zero

they remembered a wailing baby
made from stories & starlight
again & again

this was before the war turned them
against their whiter neighbors,
the browner ones, too,
before they could see god spreading
inside their enemies with impossible belonging

truth is the earth
where the window comes

the railroad rolled up
the child's tongue

it was their own grief they remembered

grief is the god
& the god filled the grief

MOTH HOLOCAUST

At night I swat small
performances of stillness
disguising beating hearts.
Each suggests a willingness
to tear my sweaters apart.
At least make me use a gun
rather than close in
with my napkin. I wish
I wasn't reminded of my son
by their streaks of golden ash.
I'm a human immune
to death's lash.
Easy to mistake dirt
for their remains —
to replace one body
with another's stains.

TO BE OR NOT

In the absence of mold
I thought I saw

Maryland — indigenous
I'm not

A horsefly, I know
Not

Would I hide
Would I live

I have not told my mom
That was yesterday and now

My mom wants to replace
The time next year

Underneath this beige lies
The house

If I were
I'd stay

Away   I could not be
I could reach the stars

The lightbulbs
Be

TO THE ONE LEFT

Whether my half-hearted maneuver
to crush you worked
I'll never know.

When I lifted
paper towel from sweater
I could see

no trace of you —
no smudge, no golden
crumble. Nada.

I shook each garment.
Scrubbed clean
the plastic surround.

I hope you still live,
despite me, burrowed
in some wooly fold.

May you leave
behind in a few
months' time

the ravaged
star-pocked remains
of your satisfaction.

SCHRÖDINGER'S SPIDER

This morning I saw him
dead on the bathroom floor —
his legs creased in parallel *L*s
& his hair of a body, still.

Relieved not to be the one
to kill him, I made of him
a poem. As I leaned closer
to admire his abdomen, he turned

— alive! Alive all along!
He seemed to yawn from a deep slumber.

Was it becoming written
that stirred him?

Or did my forgetting
what I was trained to feel
at the startle of minor notes
let me see him living?

I return to the bathroom
to find this single stroke still
there, dead, alive, decide —

BROACH: CENTO

as your own flesh
inside the spider

a small boat
uncoils

the carbon of
twilight

from our bones
— the frightening gills

backwash, feet still in
violent socks

and just by accident,
a woman wears you

MY DAUGHTER, POOPING, REQUESTS A STORY

Tell me the story of the ladybug
crossing over from summer
into the night, where the first egg
came (through the dark) & where
the tiger, snug inside his polka-dot,
peered out. Tell me the story of the raisin
squirming on the floor in search
of a door — how the knob turns
only from the other side.
Put your hand in mine.
Any story. The one about the girl
who took another girl's pencil
and wouldn't give it back.
Tell me what happened.

READING THE CREASE

My three-week-old teaches me to read
the crease between her brows
not as concern or frustration
with the state of things,
but something of this world
I've forgotten: a messianic coming
of poop. A smile's preamble.
How the dream traces
milk clouds pillowing the mouth.
Some existential crisis
mounting in the learning
to trust a body
like clockwork.

ON PERCEPTION

If you are a girl who loves her sister,
you will know her by her *rainbow eyes* —

how the colors making brown appear
side by side.

If you are a girl who loves her mother,
you will speak with pride

of her *night eyes*, when the stranger asks
and a light flickers by

your face's unblinking blue
globes — *A moth*

you will name the flying thing
ducking inside your starry coat

between the folds of what is yours
and what is someone else's

sight, thus precious,
even when, sixty years from now,

you brush from your empty breast
a loose feather that escaped the down comforter —

brush it off with panic thinking
it a moth, and your sister and mother

are both gone and living
on the side where bodies collapse

into each other's arms — where eyes fill
with sand —

eye-crystals earth-lowered
to begin again.

CROWNING VIA C-SECTION

There's no word in our culture
for the moment you arrive
bursting out my abs, sudden light
behind the paper curtain —
blood-filled version of Rukeyser's
the world would split open — a rose
enters this world, miraculous,
as slit of scissors parts sea of flesh,
your ready body lifted
from its intestinal nest. O
daughter, eyes sealed, still
dreaming of your life within,
as the nurse whisks you
past my craned neck: now I know
what Romeo must have felt
seeing that first flash of Juliet
before she disappeared
into the crowd — how futile
any attempt to stitch back
a body cut open
for love's necessary tear.
Your birth-tracks, burning there.

MEASURING UNRULY DISTANCES

I don't like you, but I love you —

My daughter flings her arms to show just how much

then whips them behind her,
taking back the mountain.

Zero is smaller than one, she reminds me.

The poet wrote that a flower blossoming beneath a flock of pigeons
helped him see the not-worth of humans.

Standing between this unit of arms
& inches of language, I see my daughter
— her pluming

a bloom
I can't count on.

BUTTERNUT SQUASH SOUP IN THE CAPITALOCENE

She is dying — each week
a different soup: butternut squash,
lobster bisque, tomato sage.
What will happen to her apartment?
My neighbor wants to know.
On the last page of the news:
a modern-day Quagga extinguished.
She is dying, and we cannot see her
dreaming of the Russian ballet
where she danced before this life:
the dream my daughter enters spinning
silver. She is dying. Each week the avocados
grow heavier. The same neighbor processes
property costs, thinking little of her heart's
breaking pumps, its smoking tree.
Maybe that's unfair of me.
Maybe he cares and prepares peppered beef broth.
They say she is dying, but I found her
sashaying in the girl's sequined dream
despite — in spite of — the Capitalocene.

regrets, upon hearing of her death

if only I brought her the dark chocolate in time

if only more pears

if only I visited

if only my last text to her wasn't

*the frittata is made of eggs, challah, cumin, milk
(in case you need to know the ingredients)*

if only I thought to plant flowers

if only her daughters came sooner

if only another year, or two days

if only more neighbors knew

if only peaches were in season

if only I could see time bend

& rear its head

if only a hand to smooth her hair

FOR ROSE ON THE AMERICAN AIRLINES FLIGHT
FROM LOS ANGELES

Your favorite ghost — daughter
who haunted your son's new apartment
when he first turned on the lamp,
stopping at her silhouette
projected in steep shadow on the north wall —

appears to me again & again
in the wrong way, as visions tend to,
especially when sprung from a fast story's soil
after takeoff, somewhere between
cloud & cloud's cotton

horizon — & I think of her image
filling the living that night
at the common flick of light
while you, still wearing those violet
tinted glasses that make me
squint to see the color of your eyes,
clutch your son's sleeve — (*It's her!*) —
in the newfound quiet of that room. Thank you

for telling me of your good friend, too,
who waits for her death
like she would a waterslide ride,
as she slips past ninety-six, wanting
"the next adventure." When we decide it's time

for you to sleep & for me to get back to work,
the sky has already dressed herself for evening
in lavender hue & one gold earring
pulsing beneath the plane's wing
carrying the pilot's soft
assurance — *Just some*
wind ahead.

ODE TO THE SUBWAY DOOR'S SCRATCHES

O thin swerves left
by bodies I'll never know. O

curves kissing the "n" of "not" —
[as in: "do not" / as in: "do not

lean on door"] — before
plunging in haphazard matte

glory skimming the metal shine
of silver panels erect with capacity

to open & close soundlessly
the black rubber river running

its partition through you,
unruly & touched too much

by fabrics, tools & limbs in rush
hours. Our motors scrape

you who becomes
you & remains left

by you: lovers / brothers, all of you,
jamming like this in unceremonious

abandon. O bastard children
of our acts of commute

you've communed here for no reason
and will later today get scrubbed away —

until then
stay.

LOSING POWER

When the power leaves our house
my husband picks up his mandolin
and plays a tune
so I make up a song —

the power, the power, we have the power,
we don't need elec-tri-ci-ty —

Our daughter laughs,
reaching for her book about farts.

We try to decipher its sentences in the dark
until we can no longer see
what's been written and what's left

is only the mandolin
and the wind
and the toilet water running.

She says *It's fun to lose power.*

I pull her close and feel on her arms
their soft eczema —
seeds rising from earth.

BLACKBERRY

meadow night's
guts

smash of river
engorged

Voldemort's good heart
(if he only knew!)

my true Jew
black with life

pimple-bushed
lucky pluck

you who sees
through all your eyes

after you turn
to tooth-caught
grain

do you still have your dream in you?

WITHOUT MY EYES I SEE

a train beneath the ocean

plane engines mimicking birds

real birds
cracking Morse code —

a truck heavy with deliveries

sprinklers doing their daily spray

more birds
climaxing in chorus

dots of furious song
despeckling
aria —

car honk

a sip of your water

leaves kissing the air &
there, a child's voice: I want to play

the sunshine with my banjo.
I want to see how it goes.

PRESENT TENSE

Today I am my sister's sister,
my father's brow,
my mother's squirm,
urging my spirit to light.

I touch my abdomen,
each daughter's doorway
opened for a few fluorescent minutes
then sewn shut
for good, if not for now.

I remain here,
even when my form bruises, blooms,
or falls away, by way of what it does
or does not say.

Instead of saying *It's getting out of hand*
won't you say *I need it in my hand*
won't you say
my hand

— a cardinal startles.
I do not mistake it for another red thing:
the flower on the soup bowl's bottom
blurred by golden croutons.

With twitch of beak & eye,
the bird returns me to any tree,
a family.

NOTES

The opening epigraph by Etel Adnan comes from her book *Time*, translated by Sarah Riggs.

"Winter Day Transcription," "The Third Year," "Age," and "An Old Testament" were written in collaboration with Noa Eini Sargent.

The title of the poem "Air holds everyone visible or not" comes from a line in Naomi Shihab Nye's poem "Ringing" (*Transfer*, 2011).

"To Be or Not" is an erasure of Kathleen Mosley's writing based on an exercise from the Hybrid Genres class in Spring 2020 at Moore College of Art & Design.

"Butternut Squash Soup in the Capitalocene" and "regrets, upon hearing of her death" are for and in memory of Pat Vitiello.

ABOUT THE AUTHOR

MAYA PINDYCK is the author of the poetry collections *Emoticoncert* (Four Way Books, 2016) and *Friend Among Stones,* winner of the Many Voices Project Award (New Rivers Press, 2009), and co-author of *A Poetry Pedagogy for Teachers* (Bloomsbury, 2022). She is the recipient of a National Endowment for the Arts Fellowship, a Poetry Society of America Chapbook Fellowship, and grants from the Historic House Trust of New York City and Abortion Conversation Projects. Her visual, collaborative, and community-based work has been exhibited at the Milton Art Bank (Milton, PA) and in New York City at the Art in Odd Places Public Festival, the Governors Island Art Fair, the Lewis H. Latimer House Museum, The Clemente, and elsewhere. Currently, Pindyck lives in Philadelphia where she is an assistant professor and director of Writing at Moore College of Art & Design. She grew up in Boston and Tel Aviv.